Sanctify
A Scriptural Novena to the Holy Spirit

by Christine Haapala
illustrated by James Reid

Suffering Servant Scriptorium
Fairfax, VA
www.sufferingservant.com

Nihil Obstat: Rev. Paul F. deLadurantaye, S.T.D.
Censor Librorum

Imprimatur: + Paul S. Lavorde
Bishop of Arlington
September 9, 2014

The *Nihil Obstat* and *Imprimatur* are official declarations that a book or pamphlet is free of doctrinal or moral error. No implication is contained therein that those who have granted the *Nihil Obstat* or *Imprimatur* agree with the contents, opinions, or statements expressed.

Verse text from the *New American Bible with Revised New Testament and Psalms* Copyright © 1991, 1986, 1970 by the Confraternity of Christian Doctrine, Washington, D.C. Used with permission. All Rights Reserved. No part of the New American Bible may be reproduced in any form without permission in writing from the copyright owner.

Illustrations are from The Life of Christ in Woodcuts, James Reid, ISBN 978-0-486-46884-6, Dover Publications, Mineola, NY. Originally published by Farrar & Rinehart, Inc., New York, 1930. Illustrations have no titles in the original work. Used with permission.

Cover design and book layout by Alison Ujueta

Copyright © 2014 Christine Haapala

ISBN: 978-0-9840394-6-3
E-book (Kindle): ISBN 978-0-9840394-7-0

All Rights Reserved.
Manufactured in the United States of America.

**Dedicated to
Immaculate Mary, Virgin Mother,
Chaste Spouse of the Holy Spirit**

Special thanks to Father Michael Duesterhaus for
his spiritual direction and encouragement.

My Dear Friends in Christ,

In this world there are more and more attempts to dismiss suffering through drugs, distractions, and ultimately government sanctioned suicide. But outside of the Faith, suffering makes no sense whatsoever. Only in following the path of Jesus Christ does suffering show a way forward. If our Lord and Savior had to suffer, how can we expect to avoid it? In a world broken by sin, suffering will be part of our lives if we pursue the path of truth and wisdom.

The first follower of Jesus was his mother Mary who also suffered - and she was not touched by Original Sin! She took on her suffering and made it an offering to the Lord.

We do not seek out punishment, but rather we accept and acknowledge that when we encounter suffering we make it a means for our own sanctification. Use these meditations well as you walk the path with our Lord and know that He is with you every step of the way.

Fr. Michael R. Duesterhaus
Priest of the Diocese of Arlington, VA

Table of Contents

Dedication Page	iii
Theological Virtues	
Day 1: Faith, Hope and Love	2
Gifts of the Holy Spirit	
Day 2: Fear of the Lord	6
Day 3: Knowledge and Piety	10
Day 4: Counsel and Fortitude	14
Day 5: Wisdom and Understanding	18
Fruit of the Holy Spirit	
Day 6: Charity, Joy and Peace	22
Day 7: Patience and Faithfulness	26
Day 8: Goodness, Generosity, Gentleness, and Kindness	30
Day 9: Modesty, Self-Control, and Chastity	34
Author's Note	38

Sanctify my Heart
A Scriptural Novena to the Holy Spirit

Day 1 - Theological Virtues: Faith, Hope and Love

Come, Holy Spirit, sanctify my heart with an increase in Faith, Hope, and Love. O My Jesus, sent by the Father to heal the brokenhearted, make my heart more like your Sacred Heart and the Immaculate Heart of your Blessed Mother. I plead for mercy, for I am a sinner. O Lord, Jesus Christ, through the shedding of your precious blood, save me and the whole world.

Elizabeth, filled with the holy Spirit, … [said to Mary], "Blessed are you who believed that what was spoken to you by the Lord would be fulfilled." … "[B]lessed are those who hear the word of God and observe it." … [T]he victory that conquers the world is our faith. *Lk 1:41,45, Lk 11:28, 1 Jn 5:4*

Sacred Heart of Jesus, formed by the Holy Spirit
in the womb of the Virgin Mother, have mercy on us.
Immaculate Heart of Mary, pierced by a sword, pray for us.

Be on your guard, stand firm in the faith. … [T]he testing of your faith produces perseverance. … "Do not let your hearts be troubled. You have faith in God; have faith also in me." … "Believe in the Lord Jesus and you and your household will be saved." *1 Cor 16:13, Jas 1:3, Jn 14:1, Acts 16:31*

Sacred Heart of Jesus, …
Immaculate Heart of Mary, …

[T]he Lord is faithful; he will strengthen you and guard you from the evil one. … In all circumstances, hold faith as a shield, to quench all [the] flaming arrows of the evil one. … [B]eloved, build yourselves up in your most holy faith; pray in the holy Spirit. *2 Thes 3:3, Eph 6:16, Jude 20*

Sacred Heart of Jesus, …
Immaculate Heart of Mary, …

For through the Spirit, by faith, we await the hope of righteousness. … [We know] that affliction produces endurance, and endurance, proven character, and proven character, hope, and hope does not disappoint. … Rejoice in hope, endure in affliction, persevere in prayer. *Gal 5:5, Rom 5:3-5, Rom 12:12*

Sacred Heart of Jesus, ...
Immaculate Heart of Mary, ...

Relieve the troubles of my heart; / bring me out of my distress. / Put an end to my affliction and my suffering. ... Our soul waits for the LORD. ... They that hope in the LORD will renew their strength, / they will soar as with eagles' wings; / They will run and not grow weary, / walk and not grow faint. *Ps 25:17-18, Ps 33:20, Is 40:31*

Sacred Heart of Jesus, ...
Immaculate Heart of Mary, ...

Though my flesh and my heart fail, / God is the rock of my heart. ... Lord, what future do I have? / You are my only hope. ... My soul, be at rest in God alone, / from whom comes my hope. ... [H]ope does not disappoint, because the love of God has been poured out in our hearts through the holy Spirit. *Ps 73:26, Ps 39:8, Ps 62:6, Rom 5:5*

Sacred Heart of Jesus, ...
Immaculate Heart of Mary, ...

What will separate us from the love of Christ? Will anguish, or distress, or persecution, or famine, or nakedness, or peril, or the sword? ... [I]t is written: / "What eye has not seen, and ear has not heard, / and what has not entered the human heart, / what God has prepared for those who love him." *Rom 8:35, 1 Cor 2:9*

Sacred Heart of Jesus, ...
Immaculate Heart of Mary, ...

[Love] bears all things, believes all things, hopes all things, endures all things. ... In return for my love they slander me,

/ even though I prayed for them. / They repay me evil for good, / hatred for my love. ... God proves his love for us in that while we were still sinners Christ died for us. *1 Cor 13:7, Ps 109:4-5, Rom 5:8*

> *Sacred Heart of Jesus, ...*
> *Immaculate Heart of Mary, ...*

[F]aith, hope, love remain, these three; but the greatest of these is love. ... God is love. ... "No one has greater love than this, to lay down one's life for one's friends." ... For God so loved the world that he gave his only Son, so that everyone who believes in him might not perish but might have eternal life. *1 Cor 13:13, 1 Jn 4:8, Jn 15:13, Jn 3:16*

> *Sacred Heart of Jesus, ...*
> *Immaculate Heart of Mary, ...*

Day 2 - Gift of the Holy Spirit: Fear of the Lord

Come, Holy Spirit, sanctify my heart with an increase in Fear of the Lord. O My Jesus, sent by the Father to heal the brokenhearted, make my heart more like your Sacred Heart and the Immaculate Heart of your Blessed Mother. I plead for mercy, for I am a sinner. O Lord, Jesus Christ, through the shedding of your precious blood, save me and the whole world.

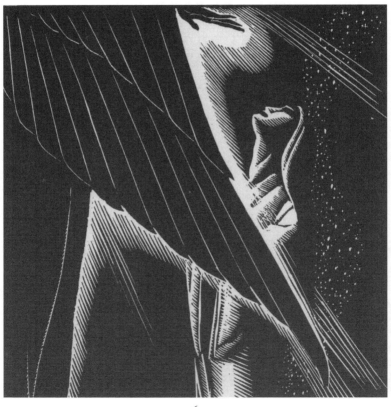

The fear of the LORD is a fountain of life. ... The beginning of wisdom is fear of the LORD, / which is formed with the faithful in the womb. ... [T]he angel said to her, "Do not be afraid, Mary, for you have found favor with God. Behold, you will conceive in your womb and bear a son, and you shall name him Jesus." *Prv 14:27, Sir 1:12, Lk 1:30-31*

*Sacred Heart of Jesus, formed by the Holy Spirit
in the womb of the Virgin Mother, have mercy on us.
Immaculate Heart of Mary, pierced by a sword, pray for us.*

Happy the man who meditates upon these things. / ... If he puts them into practice, he can cope with anything, / for the fear of the LORD is his lamp. ... Satan answered the LORD and said, "Is it for nothing that Job is God-fearing? Have you not surrounded him and his family and all that he has with your protection?" *Sir 50:28-29, Job 1:9-10*

*Sacred Heart of Jesus, ...
Immaculate Heart of Mary, ...*

Those who fear the LORD trust in the LORD, / who is their help and shield. ... Fear of the LORD leaves nothing wanting; / he who has it need seek no other support. ... No evil can harm the man who fears the LORD; / through trials, again and again he is safe. *Ps 115:11, Sir 40:26, Sir 33:1*

*Sacred Heart of Jesus, ...
Immaculate Heart of Mary, ...*

The LORD, your God, shall you fear; him shall you serve. ... Fear the LORD, you holy ones; / nothing is lacking to those who fear him. ... [K]eep the commandments of the LORD, your God, by walking in his ways and fearing him. ... He who fears the LORD is never alarmed, / never afraid; for the LORD is his hope. *Dt 6:13, Ps 34:10, Dt 8:6, Sir 34:14*

Sacred Heart of Jesus, ...
Immaculate Heart of Mary, ...

O Lord, / ... Do not abandon me in time of trouble, / in the midst of storms and dangers. ... Cast your care upon the LORD, / who will give you support. / God will never allow / the righteous to stumble. ... [F]ear the LORD and serve him completely and sincerely. ... As for me and my household, we will serve the LORD. *Sir 51:10, Ps 55:23, Jos 24:14-15*

Sacred Heart of Jesus, ...
Immaculate Heart of Mary, ...

The eyes of the LORD are upon those who love him; / he is their mighty shield and strong support, / A shelter from the heat, a shade from the noonday sun, / a guard against stumbling, a help against falling. ... The fear of God is a paradise of blessings; / its canopy, all that is glorious. *Sir 34:16, Sir 40:27*

Sacred Heart of Jesus, ...
Immaculate Heart of Mary, ...

[T]he God of Daniel is to be reverenced and feared: / "For he is the living God, enduring forever; / his kingdom shall not be destroyed, / and his dominion shall be without end." ... "You who fear the LORD, give praise!" ... Let all the earth fear the LORD; / let all who dwell in the world show reverence. *Dan 6:27, Ps 22:24, Ps 33:8*

Sacred Heart of Jesus, ...
Immaculate Heart of Mary, ...

Trust in the LORD with all your heart, / … fear the LORD and turn away from evil. … Fear God and keep his commandments, for this is man's all; because God will bring to judgment every work, with all its hidden qualities, whether good or bad. *Prv 3:5,7, Ecc 12:13*

> *Sacred Heart of Jesus, …*
> *Immaculate Heart of Mary, …*

[The thief on the cross said], "Have you no fear of God, for you are subject to the same condemnation?" … Then he said, "Jesus, remember me when you come into your kingdom." … Blessed are they who wash their robes so as to have the right to the tree of life and enter the city through its gates. *Lk 23:40,42, Rv 22:14*

> *Sacred Heart of Jesus, …*
> *Immaculate Heart of Mary, …*

Day 3 - Gifts of the Holy Spirit: Knowledge and Piety

Come, Holy Spirit, sanctify my heart with an increase in Knowledge and Piety. O My Jesus, sent by the Father to heal the brokenhearted, make my heart more like your Sacred Heart and the Immaculate Heart of your Blessed Mother. I plead for mercy, for I am a sinner. O Lord, Jesus Christ, through the shedding of your precious blood, save me and the whole world.

Is not your piety a source of confidence, / and your integrity of life your hope? … "God resists the proud, / but gives grace to the humble." … Mary said: "Behold, I am the handmaid of the Lord. … For he has looked upon his handmaid's lowliness; / behold, from now on will all ages call me blessed." *Job 4:6, Jas 4:6, Lk 1:38,48*

> *Sacred Heart of Jesus, formed by the Holy Spirit*
> *in the womb of the Virgin Mother, have mercy on us.*
> *Immaculate Heart of Mary, pierced by a sword, pray for us.*

[H]umility goes before honors. … Strive … for that holiness without which no one will see the Lord. … Receive … knowledge rather than choice gold. … [M]ake every effort to supplement your faith with virtue, virtue with knowledge. *Prv 15:33, Heb 12:14, Prv 8:10, 2 Pt 1:5*

> *Sacred Heart of Jesus, ...*
> *Immaculate Heart of Mary, ...*

Oh, the depths of the riches and wisdom and knowledge of God! How inscrutable are his judgments and how unsearchable his ways! … For the LORD gives wisdom, / from his mouth come knowledge and understanding; … knowledge will please your soul. *Rom 11:33, Prv 2:6,10*

> *Sacred Heart of Jesus, ...*
> *Immaculate Heart of Mary, ...*

[W]e do not cease praying for you and asking that you may be filled with the knowledge of his will through all spiritual wisdom and understanding to live in a manner worthy of the Lord, so as to be fully pleasing, in every good work bearing fruit and growing in the knowledge of God. *Col 1:9-10*

Sacred Heart of Jesus, ...
Immaculate Heart of Mary, ...

[R]eturn to me with your whole heart, / with fasting, and weeping, and mourning; / Rend your hearts ... proclaim a fast. ... I turned to the Lord God, pleading in earnest prayer, with fasting, sackcloth, and ashes. I prayed to the LORD, my God and confessed. *Joel 2:12-13,15, Dan 9:3-4*

Sacred Heart of Jesus, ...
Immaculate Heart of Mary, ...

[I]f my people ... humble themselves and pray, and seek my presence and turn from their evil ways, I will hear them from heaven and pardon their sins and revive their land. ... [Y]our prayer has been heard and your almsgiving remembered before God. *2 Chr 7:14, Acts 10:31*

Sacred Heart of Jesus, ...
Immaculate Heart of Mary, ...

Give to the LORD the glory due God's name. / Bow down before the LORD's holy splendor. ... I kneel before the Father ... to know the love of Christ that surpasses knowledge. ... I call on your name, O LORD, / from the bottom of the pit. / .... You defended me in mortal danger, / you redeemed my life. *Ps 29:2, Eph 3:14,19, Lam 3:55,58*

Sacred Heart of Jesus, ...
Immaculate Heart of Mary, ...

Say to God: "How awesome your deeds!" / ... All on earth fall in worship before you. ... [L]et us bow down in worship; / let us kneel before the LORD who made us. ... "It is written: / 'You shall worship the Lord, your God, / and him alone shall you serve.'" *Ps 66:3-4, Ps 95:6, Lk 4:8*

Sacred Heart of Jesus, ...
Immaculate Heart of Mary, ...

[Jesus] began to teach them ... / "Blessed are they who hunger and thirst for righteousness, / ... Blessed are they who are persecuted for the sake of righteousness, / for theirs is the kingdom of heaven." ... [E]ven if you should suffer because of righteousness, blessed are you. *Mt 5:2,6,10, 1 Pt 3:14*

Sacred Heart of Jesus, ...
Immaculate Heart of Mary, ...

Day 4 - Gifts of the Holy Spirit: Counsel and Fortitude

Come, Holy Spirit, sanctify my heart with an increase in Counsel and Fortitude. O My Jesus, sent by the Father to heal the brokenhearted, make my heart more like your Sacred Heart and the Immaculate Heart of your Blessed Mother. I plead for mercy, for I am a sinner. O Lord, Jesus Christ, through the shedding of your precious blood, save me and the whole world.

Mary kept all these things, reflecting on them in her heart. … Simeon blessed them and said to Mary … "you yourself a sword will pierce." … Standing by the cross of Jesus were his mother. … For whenever anyone bears the pain of unjust suffering because of consciousness of God, that is a grace. *Lk 2:19,34,35, Jn 19:25, 1 Pt 2:19*

> *Sacred Heart of Jesus, formed by the Holy Spirit*
> *in the womb of the Virgin Mother, have mercy on us.*
> *Immaculate Heart of Mary, pierced by a sword, pray for us.*

Hear my cry for help, / …. To you I pray, O LORD; / at dawn you will hear my cry. … Be brave and steadfast; do not fear or lose heart. … My strength and my courage is the LORD, … In your mercy you led the people you redeemed; / in your strength you guided them to your holy dwelling. *Ps 5:3-4, 1 Chr 22:13, Ex 15:2,13*

> *Sacred Heart of Jesus, …*
> *Immaculate Heart of Mary, …*

I bless the LORD who counsels me; / even at night my heart exhorts me. / I keep the LORD always before me; / with the LORD at my right, I shall never be shaken. … The counsel of the LORD belongs to the faithful; / … My eyes are ever upon the LORD, / who frees my feet from the snare. *Ps 16:7-8, Ps 25:14-15*

> *Sacred Heart of Jesus, …*
> *Immaculate Heart of Mary, …*

My life is worn out by sorrow, / my years by sighing. / My strength fails in affliction. … But I trust in you, LORD; / I say, "You are my God." … For what man knows God's

counsel, / or who can conceive what the LORD intends?
Ps 31:11,15, Wis 9:13

Sacred Heart of Jesus, ...
Immaculate Heart of Mary, ...

Who has cupped in his hand the waters of the sea? ... The LORD is the eternal God. / ... He gives strength to the fainting. ... He will renew your strength, / and you shall be like a watered garden, / like a spring whose water never fails. *Is 40:12,28-29, Is 58:11*

Sacred Heart of Jesus, ...
Immaculate Heart of Mary, ...

When I cried out, you answered; / you strengthened my spirit. ... [B]e not dismayed; I am your God. / I will strengthen you, and help you, / and uphold you with my right hand of justice. ... I will instruct you and show you the way you should walk, / give you counsel and watch over you. *Ps 138:3, Is 41:10, Ps 32:8*

Sacred Heart of Jesus, ...
Immaculate Heart of Mary, ...

At this I weep, / my eyes run with tears: / Far from me are all who could console me. ... Be brave and steadfast; have no fear or dread of them, for it is the LORD, your God, who marches with you; he will never fail you or forsake you. ... Happy those who do not follow / the counsel of the wicked, / Nor go the way of sinners. *Lam 1:16, Dt 31:6, Ps 1:1*

Sacred Heart of Jesus, ...
Immaculate Heart of Mary, ...

The Pharisees went out and immediately took counsel with the Herodians against him to put him to death. ... For Christ also suffered for sins once, the righteous for the sake of the unrighteous, that he might lead you to God. ... [A]s you share in the sufferings, you also share in the encouragement. *Mk 3:6, 1 Pt 3:18, 2 Cor 1:7*

> *Sacred Heart of Jesus, ...*
> *Immaculate Heart of Mary, ...*

Why, then, should you forget us, / abandon us so long a time? ... May the Lord direct your hearts to ... the endurance of Christ. ... At noon darkness came over the whole land until three in the afternoon. ... Jesus gave a loud cry and breathed his last. ... "They will look upon him whom they have pierced." *Lam 5:20, 2 Thes 3:5, Mk 15:33,37, Jn 19:37*

> *Sacred Heart of Jesus, ...*
> *Immaculate Heart of Mary, ...*

Day 5 - Gifts of the Holy Spirit: Wisdom and Understanding

Come, Holy Spirit, sanctify my heart with an increase in Wisdom and Understanding. O My Jesus, sent by the Father to heal the brokenhearted, make my heart more like your Sacred Heart and the Immaculate Heart of your Blessed Mother. I plead for mercy, for I am a sinner. O Lord, Jesus Christ, through the shedding of your precious blood, save me and the whole world.

Before all things else wisdom was created; / and prudent understanding from eternity. ... [T]he genealogy of Jesus Christ, the son of David, the son of Abraham. ... David became the father of Solomon, whose mother had been the wife of Uriah. ... Joseph, the husband of Mary. Of her was born Jesus who is called the Messiah. *Sir 1:4, Mt 1:1,6,16*

Sacred Heart of Jesus, formed by the Holy Spirit
in the womb of the Virgin Mother, have mercy on us.
Immaculate Heart of Mary, pierced by a sword, pray for us.

Whence, then, comes wisdom, / and where is the place of understanding? ... God said, "Ask something of me and I will give it to you." Solomon answered: ... "Give your servant, therefore, an understanding heart to judge your people." ... I pleaded, and the spirit of Wisdom came to me. *Job 28:20, 1 Kgs 3:5-6,9, Wis 7:7*

Sacred Heart of Jesus, ...
Immaculate Heart of Mary, ...

Happy the man who meditates on wisdom, / and reflects on knowledge; / ... and understands her paths. ... Wisdom delivered from tribulations those who served her. ... [T]he whole world sought audience with Solomon, to hear from him the wisdom which God had put in his heart. *Sir 14:20-21, Wis 10:9, 1 Kgs 10:24*

Sacred Heart of Jesus, ...
Immaculate Heart of Mary, ...

[F]ear of the LORD is wisdom; / and avoiding evil is understanding. ... Does not Wisdom call, / and Understanding raise her voice? ... Receive my instruction in preference to silver. ... Wisdom is better than corals. ... Teach us to count our days aright, / that we may gain wisdom of heart. ... If you desire wisdom keep the commandments, / and the LORD will bestow her upon you. *Job 28:28, Prv 8:1,10-11, Ps 90:12, Sir 1:23*

Sacred Heart of Jesus, ...
Immaculate Heart of Mary, ...

Have no anxiety at all ... make your requests known to God. Then, the peace of God that surpasses all understanding will guard your hearts and minds in Christ Jesus. ... [W]e do not cease praying for you and asking that you may be filled with the knowledge of his will through all spiritual wisdom and understanding. *Phil 4:6-7, Col 1:9*

Sacred Heart of Jesus, ...
Immaculate Heart of Mary, ...

I have dealt with great things that I do not understand; / things too wonderful for me, which I cannot know. / I had heard of you by word of mouth, / but now my eye has seen you. ... And thus were the paths of those on earth made straight, / and men learned what was your pleasure, / and were saved by Wisdom. *Job 42:3-5, Wis 9:18*

Sacred Heart of Jesus, ...
Immaculate Heart of Mary, ...

Though the snares of the wicked surround me, / your teaching I do not forget. ... Teach me wisdom and knowledge, / for in your commands I trust. ... Search [Wisdom] out, discover her; seek her and you will find her. / Then when you have her, do not let her go. ... For where your treasure is, there also will your heart be. *Ps 119:61,66, Sir 6:28, Mt 6:21*

Sacred Heart of Jesus, ...
Immaculate Heart of Mary, ...

Resplendent and unfading is Wisdom, / and she is readily perceived by those who love her, / and found by those who seek her. ... He will pour forth his words of wisdom / and in prayer give thanks to the LORD. ... Jesus advanced [in] wisdom and age and favor before God and man. *Wis 6:12, Sir 39:6, Lk 2:52*

Sacred Heart of Jesus, ...
Immaculate Heart of Mary, ...

After three days [Joseph and Mary] found [Jesus] in the temple, sitting in the midst of the teachers, listening to them and asking them questions. ... "[T]here is something greater than Solomon here." ... He began to teach them that the Son of Man must suffer greatly and be rejected ... be killed, and rise after three days. *Lk 2:46, Mt 12:42, Mk 8:31*

Sacred Heart of Jesus, ...
Immaculate Heart of Mary, ...

Day 6 - Fruit of the Holy Spirit: Charity, Joy and Peace

Come, Holy Spirit, sanctify my heart with an increase in Charity, Joy and Peace. O My Jesus, sent by the Father to heal the brokenhearted, make my heart more like your Sacred Heart and the Immaculate Heart of your Blessed Mother. I plead for mercy, for I am a sinner. O Lord, Jesus Christ, through the shedding of your precious blood, save me and the whole world.

[T]he fruit of the Spirit is love, joy, peace. ... The angel said ... "I proclaim to you good news of great joy." ... For a child is born to us ... Prince of Peace. / His dominion is vast / and forever peaceful. ... [The magi] were overjoyed at seeing the star, and on entering the house they saw the child with Mary his mother. *Gal 5:22, Lk 2:10, Is 9:5-6, Mt 2:10-11*

> *Sacred Heart of Jesus, formed by the Holy Spirit*
> *in the womb of the Virgin Mother, have mercy on us.*
> *Immaculate Heart of Mary, pierced by a sword, pray for us.*

There is an appointed time for everything, / ... a time to laugh ... A time to love, ... a time of peace. ... The LORD, your God, is in your midst / ... He will rejoice over you with gladness, / and renew you in his love. ... The King of Israel, the LORD, is in your midst; / you have no further misfortune to fear. *Ecc 3:1,4,8, Zep 3:17, Zep 3:15*

> *Sacred Heart of Jesus, ...*
> *Immaculate Heart of Mary, ...*

Rejoice always. Pray without ceasing. In all circumstances give thanks. ... [P]ursue righteousness, faith, love, and peace, along with those who call on the Lord with purity of heart. ... For the kingdom of God ... [is] righteousness, peace, and joy in the holy Spirit. *1 Thes 5:16-18, 2 Tm 2:22, Rom 14:17*

> *Sacred Heart of Jesus, ...*
> *Immaculate Heart of Mary, ...*

Consider it all joy, my brothers, when you encounter various trials. ... Those whom the LORD has ransomed ... will meet with joy and gladness, / sorrow and mourning will flee. ... [Love] rejoices with the truth. It bears all things, believes all

things, hopes all things, endures all things. Love never fails. … I rejoice in the LORD / … God, my Lord, is my strength.
Jas 1:2, Is 35:10, 1 Cor 13:6-8, Hab 3:18-19

> *Sacred Heart of Jesus, …*
> *Immaculate Heart of Mary, …*

How long must I carry sorrow in my soul, / grief in my heart? … Grant my heart joy in your help. … Those who sow in tears / will reap with cries of joy. … "Do not be saddened this day, for rejoicing in the LORD must be your strength!" … I will turn the mourning into joy, / I will console and gladden them after their sorrows. *Ps 13:3,6, Ps 126:5, Neh 8:10, Jer 31:13*

> *Sacred Heart of Jesus, …*
> *Immaculate Heart of Mary, …*

Deceit is in the hands of those who plot evil, / but those who counsel peace have joy. … Rejoice not over me, O my enemy! / though I have fallen, I will arise; / though I sit in darkness, the LORD is my light. … In peace I shall both lie down and sleep, / for you alone, LORD, make me secure. *Prv 12:20, Mi 7:8, Ps 4:9*

> *Sacred Heart of Jesus, …*
> *Immaculate Heart of Mary, …*

[M]y prayer will be heard. / God will give me freedom and peace / from those who war against me, / though there are many who oppose me. … [L]ive in peace, and the God of love and peace will be with you. … "Blessed are the peacemakers, / for they will be called children of God." *Ps 55:18-19, 2 Cor 13:11, Mt 5:9*

Sacred Heart of Jesus, ...
Immaculate Heart of Mary, ...

"Peace I leave with you; my peace I give to you. ... If you loved me, you would rejoice that I am going to the Father." ... "I have told you this so that my joy may be in you and your joy may be complete. ... No one has greater love than this, to lay down one's life for one's friends." *Jn 14:27-28, Jn 15:11,13*

Sacred Heart of Jesus, ...
Immaculate Heart of Mary, ...

For the sake of the joy that lay before him he endured the cross. ... [Jesus] said, "It is finished." And bowing his head, he handed over the spirit. ... [T]hey went away quickly from the tomb, fearful yet overjoyed. ... "Peace be with you. As the Father has sent me, so I send you." *Heb 12:2, Jn 19:30, Mt 28:8, Jn 20:21*

Sacred Heart of Jesus, ...
Immaculate Heart of Mary, ...

Day 7 - Fruit of the Holy Spirit: Patience and Faithfulness

Come, Holy Spirit, sanctify my heart with an increase in Patience and Faithfulness. O My Jesus, sent by the Father to heal the brokenhearted, make my heart more like your Sacred Heart and the Immaculate Heart of your Blessed Mother. I plead for mercy, for I am a sinner. O Lord, Jesus Christ, through the shedding of your precious blood, save me and the whole world.

[W]hen the fullness of time had come, God sent his Son, born of a woman, born under the law, to ransom those under the law. ... Joseph too went up... to the city of David that is called Bethlehem ... to be enrolled with Mary, his betrothed, who was with child. ... She ... laid [Jesus] in a manger, because there was no room for them in the inn. *Gal 4:4-5, Lk 2:4-5,7*

Sacred Heart of Jesus, formed by the Holy Spirit
in the womb of the Virgin Mother, have mercy on us.
Immaculate Heart of Mary, pierced by a sword, pray for us.

What strength have I that I should endure, / and what is my limit that I should be patient? ... [I]f you are patient when you suffer for doing what is good, this is a grace before God. ... [P]ursue righteousness, devotion, faith, love, patience. ... Be patient ... until the coming of the Lord. ... [W]e call blessed those who have persevered. *Job 6:11, 1 Pt 2:20, 1 Tm 6:11, Jas 5:7,11*

Sacred Heart of Jesus, ...
Immaculate Heart of Mary, ...

I do not fear. / What can mere flesh do to me? ... Be still before the LORD; / wait for God. ... I waited, waited for the LORD; / who bent down and heard my cry. ... You listen, LORD, to the needs of the poor; / you encourage them and hear their prayers. *Ps 56:5, Ps 37:7, Ps 40:2, Ps 10:17*

Sacred Heart of Jesus, ...
Immaculate Heart of Mary, ...

[I]f we hope for what we do not see, we wait with endurance. ... With all prayer and supplication, pray at every opportunity in the Spirit. ... [B]e watchful with all

perseverance. ... Accept whatever befalls you, / in crushing misfortune be patient; / ... Trust God and he will help you.
Rom 8:25, Eph 6:18, Sir 2:4,6

> *Sacred Heart of Jesus, ...*
> *Immaculate Heart of Mary, ...*

How long, O LORD? I cry for help. ...Why do you let me see ruin; / why must I look at misery? ... Rejoice in hope, endure in affliction, persevere in prayer. ... [We] boast of you in the churches of God regarding your endurance and faith in all your persecutions and the afflictions you endure.
Hab 1:2-3, Rom 12:12, 2 Thes 1:4

> *Sacred Heart of Jesus, ...*
> *Immaculate Heart of Mary, ...*

I will give them a heart with which to understand that I am the LORD. ... [W]e walk by faith, not by sight. ... [W]e are surrounded by so great a cloud of witnesses, let us rid ourselves of every burden and sin that clings to us and persevere in running the race. ... I have finished the race; I have kept the faith. *Jer 24:7, 2 Cor 5:7, Heb 12:1, 2 Tm 4:7*

> *Sacred Heart of Jesus, ...*
> *Immaculate Heart of Mary, ...*

God is faithful and will not let you be tried beyond your strength; but with the trial he will also provide a way out. ... LORD, hear my prayer; / in your faithfulness listen to my pleading; / ... destroy all who attack me, / for I am your servant. ... [P]ersecutions, and sufferings ... Yet from all these things the Lord delivered me. *1 Cor 10:13, Ps 143:1,12, 2 Tm 3:11*

Sacred Heart of Jesus, ...
Immaculate Heart of Mary, ...

The LORD is close to the brokenhearted, / saves those whose spirit is crushed. / Many are the troubles of the just, / but the LORD delivers from them all. ... [L]et perseverance be perfect, so that you may be perfect. ... You will be hated by all because of my name, but whoever endures till the end will be saved. *Ps 34:19-20, Jas 1:4, Mt 10:22*

Sacred Heart of Jesus, ...
Immaculate Heart of Mary, ...

I live by faith in the Son of God who has loved me and given himself up for me. ... [W]hen they came to Jesus and saw that he was already dead ... one soldier thrust his lance into his side, and immediately blood and water flowed out. ... Give thanks to God, bless his name; / ... whose faithfulness lasts through every age. *Gal 2:20, Jn 19:33-34, Ps 100:4-5*

Sacred Heart of Jesus, ...
Immaculate Heart of Mary, ...

Day 8 - Fruit of the Holy Spirit: Goodness, Generosity, Gentleness and Kindness

Come, Holy Spirit, sanctify my heart with an increase in Goodness, Generosity, Gentleness and Kindness. O My Jesus, sent by the Father to heal the brokenhearted, make my heart more like your Sacred Heart and the Immaculate Heart of your Blessed Mother. I plead for mercy, for I am a sinner. O Lord, Jesus Christ, through the shedding of your precious blood, save me and the whole world.

Does he not see my ways, / and number all my steps? / … Does not the same One fashion us before our birth?… [Jesus] went down with [Mary and Joseph] and came to Nazareth, and was obedient to them; and his mother kept all these things in her heart. … "Can anything good come from Nazareth?" *Job 31:4,15, Lk 2:51, Jn 1:46*

Sacred Heart of Jesus, formed by the Holy Spirit
in the womb of the Virgin Mother, have mercy on us.
Immaculate Heart of Mary, pierced by a sword, pray for us.

Trust God, / … hope for good things. … Good and upright is the LORD, / who shows sinners the way. … Have mercy on me, God, in your goodness; / in your abundant compassion blot out my offense. … How great is your goodness, LORD, / stored up for those who fear you. *Sir 2:6,9, Ps 25:8, Ps 51:3, Ps 31:20*

Sacred Heart of Jesus, …
Immaculate Heart of Mary, …

[Y]ou shall love the LORD, your God, with all your heart. … Learn to savor how good the LORD is; / happy are those who take refuge in him. … Live as children of light, for light produces every kind of goodness and righteousness and truth. … The LORD loves justice and right / and fills the earth with goodness. *Dt 6:5, Ps 34:9, Eph 5:8-9, Ps 33:5*

Sacred Heart of Jesus, …
Immaculate Heart of Mary, …

God, in your great kindness answer me / with your constant help. / Rescue me from the mire; / do not let me sink. / Rescue me from my enemies. … Do not let the floodwaters overwhelm me. ... Answer me, LORD in your generous love. *Ps 69:14-17*

Sacred Heart of Jesus, ...
Immaculate Heart of Mary, ...

LORD, do not withhold your compassion from me. ... For all about me are evils beyond count. ... You are my help and deliverer; / my God, do not delay! ... Show me your compassion that I may live. ... Your compassion is great, O LORD; / in accord with your edicts give me life. *Ps 40:12-13,18, Ps 119:77,156*

Sacred Heart of Jesus, ...
Immaculate Heart of Mary, ...

[M]ay your enduring kindness ever preserve me. ... Put to shame and confound / all who seek to take my life. ... Give thanks to the LORD, for he is good, / for his kindness endures forever. ... Only goodness and love will pursue me / all the days of my life; / I will dwell in the house of the LORD / for years to come. *Ps 40:12,15, 1 Chr 16:34, Ps 23:6*

Sacred Heart of Jesus, ...
Immaculate Heart of Mary, ...

I, the LORD, bring about kindness, / justice and uprightness on the earth. ... The LORD is gracious and merciful, / slow to anger and abounding in love. / The LORD is good to all. ... The LORD, the LORD, a merciful and gracious God, slow to anger and rich in kindness and fidelity, continuing his kindness for a thousand generations. *Jer 9:23, Ps 145:8-9, Ex 34:6-7*

Sacred Heart of Jesus, ...
Immaculate Heart of Mary, ...

"Can anything good come from Nazareth?" Philip said to him, "Come and see." ... Give thanks to the LORD, for he is good, / for his kindness endures forever. ... "Hosanna to the Son of David; / blessed is he who comes in the name of the Lord." ... "This is Jesus the prophet, from Nazareth in Galilee." *Jn 1:46, 1 Chr 16:34, Mt 21:9,11*

Sacred Heart of Jesus, ...
Immaculate Heart of Mary, ...

At dawn let me hear of your kindness, / for in you I trust. / Show me the path I should walk. ... "Then come, follow me." ... [C]arrying the cross himself he went out to ... Golgotha. ... Pilate also had an inscription written and put on the cross. It read, "Jesus the Nazorean, the King of the Jews." *Ps 143:8, Mt 19:21, Jn 19:17,19*

Sacred Heart of Jesus, ...
Immaculate Heart of Mary, ...

Day 9 - Fruit of the Holy Spirit: Modesty, Self-Control, and Chastity

Come, Holy Spirit, sanctify my heart with an increase in Modesty, Self-Control, and Chastity. O My Jesus, sent by the Father to heal the brokenhearted, make my heart more like your Sacred Heart and the Immaculate Heart of your Blessed Mother. I plead for mercy, for I am a sinner. O Lord, Jesus Christ, through the shedding of your precious blood, save me and the whole world.

In the beginning was the Word ... And the Word became flesh / and made his dwelling among us. ... [B]y sending his own Son in the likeness of sinful flesh and for the sake of sin, he condemned sin in the flesh. ... The spirit of the Lord GOD is upon me, / ... He has sent me ... to heal the brokenhearted. *Jn 1:1,14, Rom 8:3, Is 61:1*

> *Sacred Heart of Jesus, formed by the Holy Spirit*
> *in the womb of the Virgin Mother, have mercy on us.*
> *Immaculate Heart of Mary, pierced by a sword, pray for us.*

[B]eloved, since you await these things, be eager to be found without spot or blemish before him, at peace. ... The LORD loves the pure of heart. ... "Blessed are the clean of heart, / for they will see God." ... [T]he angel Gabriel was sent from God ... to a virgin ... Mary. ... [H]e said, "Hail, favored one! The Lord is with you." *2 Pt 3:14, Prv 22:11, Mt 5:8, Lk 1:26-28*

> *Sacred Heart of Jesus, ...*
> *Immaculate Heart of Mary, ...*

[O]ffer your bodies as a living sacrifice, holy and pleasing to God your spiritual worship. Do not conform yourselves to this age. ... [S]he will be saved through motherhood, provided women persevere in faith and love and holiness, with self-control. ... [M]ake every effort to supplement your faith with virtue ... knowledge with self-control. *Rom 12:1-2, 1 Tm 2:15, 2 Pt 1:5-6*

> *Sacred Heart of Jesus, ...*
> *Immaculate Heart of Mary, ...*

Immorality or any impurity or greed must not even be mentioned among you, as is fitting among holy ones, no obscenity or silly or suggestive talk, which is out of place, but instead, thanksgiving. ... You changed my mourning into dancing; / ... O LORD, my God, / forever will I give you thanks. *Eph 5:3-4, Ps 30:12-13*

> *Sacred Heart of Jesus, ...*
> *Immaculate Heart of Mary, ...*

[M]y only friend is darkness. ... [R]emember that the days of darkness will be many. ... [D]o not get drunk on wine, in which lies debauchery, but be filled with the Spirit, addressing one another [in] psalms and hymns to the Lord in your hearts. ... [L]ive soberly. ... [L]et us stay alert and sober. ... Do not quench the Spirit. *Ps 88:19, Ecc 11:8, Eph 5:18-19, 1Pt 1:13, 1 Thes 5:6,19*

> *Sacred Heart of Jesus, ...*
> *Immaculate Heart of Mary, ...*

[I]n everything we commend ourselves as ministers of God, through much endurance, in afflictions, hardships, constraints, beatings, imprisonments, riots, labors, vigils, fasts; by purity, knowledge, patience, kindness, in a holy spirit, in unfeigned love, in truthful speech, in the power of God. *2 Cor 6:4-7*

> *Sacred Heart of Jesus, ...*
> *Immaculate Heart of Mary, ...*

Watch carefully then how you live, not as foolish persons. ...This is the will of God, your holiness: that you refrain from immorality. ... For God did not call us to impurity but to holiness. ... [S]trengthen your hearts, to be blameless in holiness before our God and Father. ... Pray without ceasing. *Eph 5:15, 1 Thes 4:3,7, 1 Thes 3:13, 1 Thes 5:17*

Sacred Heart of Jesus, ...
Immaculate Heart of Mary, ...

"Behold, the Lamb of God, who takes away the sin of the world." ... [Y]ou were ransomed from your futile conduct ... with the precious blood of Christ as of a spotless unblemished lamb. ... It was fitting that we should have such a high priest: holy, innocent, undefiled, separated from sinners, higher than the heavens. *Jn 1:29, 1 Pt 1:18-19, Heb 7:26*

Sacred Heart of Jesus, ...
Immaculate Heart of Mary, ...

[H]e surrendered himself to death / and was counted among the wicked. ... The lamb must be ... without blemish [and] slaughtered during the evening twilight. ... [T]he veil of the sanctuary was torn in two from top to bottom. The earth quaked. ..."Worthy is the Lamb that was slain / to receive power and riches, wisdom and strength, / honor and glory and blessing." *Is 53:12, Ex 12:5-6, Mt 27:51, Rv 5:12*

Sacred Heart of Jesus, ...
Immaculate Heart of Mary, ...

Author's Note

Dearest Friends in Christ:

At times we pass through deep, dark valleys - places of suffering and isolation. In the valley we may feel alone, but Jesus Christ is present there. The presence of Christ in this valley is only visible when we lay our suffering at the foot of his cross. It is in this release that we find a certain joy in sharing in the salvific sacrifice. Our Blessed Mother assists us in this abandonment to God's will.

In that dark valley, I wrote this book. Many years ago, I was asked to write a prayer book that a priest could share with someone who was in hospice, prison, or was suffering deeply. For years I just focused on the suffering, trying at length to itemize all the sufferings we may endure. Flood, famine, plague come to mind, but I was on the wrong track. Sacred Scriptures tell us "[L]ook and see / Whether there is there any suffering like my suffering…" *Lam 1:12* I have always seen Mary in those words. How could she endure the pain of the cross – the piercing of her heart with the sword that pierced her Son's heart? The answer is Grace. She who is "full of grace" endures every suffering – her Son's and ours.

By setting aside the suffering of all, I entered that lonely valley of personal suffering that no one can understand or relieve, but God. God's mighty hand holds us to his heart – his Love, which is the Holy Spirit and we find solace. St. Paul encourages us often in his letters to "pray always" and "pray without ceasing". This prayer book, which is my tenth, provides a Scriptural interlude of nine days to focus on the graces that the Holy Spirit gives us, if we are only open to receive them and grow them. This book begins – with Faith, the first of the three Theological Virtues. We step out in Faith, though there is suffering, darkness and turmoil all around. Through reflective and meditative selections from Sacred Scripture, this daily journey encounters the Theological Virtues

[*Faith, Hope, Love*], the Gifts of the Holy Spirit [*Fear of the Lord, Knowledge, Piety, Counsel, Fortitude, Wisdom and Understanding*], and the Fruit of the Holy Spirit [*Charity, Joy, Peace, Patience, Faithfulness, Goodness, Generosity, Gentleness, Kindness, Modesty, Self-Control, and Chastity*]. This novena is an offering up of suffering by seeking the Lord's gracious assistance. Grace needs watering through the spring of prayer and nurturing through the constant practice of the grace we are given. The perfection found in grace and the resulting solace does not happen overnight. It will not happen in nine days, or maybe not even in a year. It is a spiritual journey, where the destination is Heaven. Through the power of the Holy Spirit, Jesus Christ became man, born of the Virgin Mary. Christ was sent by the Father to heal the brokenhearted. Jesus took on all the brokenness and sufferings of humanity through his passion and death on the cross. Little by little, our heart is transformed into a new creation through our imitation of the Sacred Heart of Jesus and the Immaculate Heart of Mary.

Every word of this manuscript was written in tears and in the Adoration Chapel before the Living God – truly Present. I hope and pray that through these words, you emerge from any dark valley of suffering and solitude you find yourself in. I pray that you find solace in the perfection of the Heavenly Father, the hearts of Jesus and Mary.

To Jesus through Mary,
Christine
February 17, 2014

In the fiftieth year of the founding of
Holy Spirit Catholic Church
Annandale, Virginia

Products from Suffering Servant Scriptorium

PRAYER BOOKS FOR CHILDREN OF ALL AGES

Speak, Lord, I am Listening A Rosary Book (2nd Ed, with Luminous Mysteries. Includes Study and Discussion Guide.) This prayer book presents the richness of the Sacred Mysteries of the Most Holy Rosary in terms that children can visualize and understand. Gus Muller's watercolors use the full palette of color expression to explore the depths of the agony of Christ crucified and reach the heights of the Blessed Virgin Mary's glorious reign as Queen of Heaven and Earth. Succinct and most apt meditation selections yield a wealth of spiritual insight into the mysterious events of the lives of Jesus and Mary. The Scriptures and watercolor illustrations coupled with the prayers of the Most Holy Rosary provide a rich meditation platform for teaching prayer and devotion to Jesus and Mary.

Follow Me A Stations of the Cross Book. Inspired watercolors and selections of God's Word introduce children to the suffering of our Savior Jesus Christ by walking each step with Him to Calvary. Along with each station is a heroically holy person who epitomized self-sacrifice and was beatified or canonized by Pope John Paul II.

PRAYER BOOKS FOR ADULTS AND TEENAGERS

Pearls of Peace Spiritually walk in Jesus' footsteps by praying the mysteries of the Most Holy Rosary and meditating on the accompanying Holy Land photography. Follow the Holy Family from Bethlehem to Nazareth to Jerusalem. Walk with Jesus, his Blessed Mother, and his disciples to places, such as, Cana, the Sea of Galilee, Mount of Temptation, Mount Tabor, Garden of Gethsemane, Via Dolorosa, and Calvary. In her ninth Scriptural prayer book, Christine Haapala reveals another view of the mysteries of the Most Holy Rosary through meditations from the Gospels and the Epistles of St. Paul. This book is enriched by the stunning photography of Rev. Gary Coulter, Diocese of Lincoln, who led two pilgrimages to the Holy Land and documented these spirit-filled journeys through photography.

In His Presence: Seven Visits to the Blessed Sacrament This meditation book outlines SEVEN VISITS to the Blessed Sacrament. This prayer book can be used in one evening, such as, during the Holy Thursday

Seven Church Pilgrimage. It can be used for seven consecutive days for a special prayer request. And, it can be used periodically, whenever you can spend time visiting Jesus in the Blessed Sacrament.

The Suffering Servant's Courage (2nd Ed, with Luminous Mysteries) This prayer book integrates poignant Sacred Scripture verses about courage and fortitude, the prayers of the Most Holy Rosary, and illustrations from the inspired artistry of the 19th century Catholic illustrator Gustave Dore.

Seraphim and Cherubim A Scriptural Chaplet of the Holy Angels. Angels have been with us since the beginning in the "Garden of Eden" and will be with us at the "End of Age." This prayer book joins together Sacred Scripture selections with special invocations to our Blessed Mother and the Holy Archangels. This book includes fabulous full-color pictures from the masters, such as, Raphael, Bruegel the Elder, Perugino and many others. It also includes a newly composed Novena of the Holy Angels and the traditional Litany of the Holy Angels. Those who pray without ceasing and ponder the Good News will find this book equally inspiring and encouraging.

Psalter of Jesus and Mary This pocket-size Scriptural Rosary prayer book includes the 150 Psalms Scriptural Rosary for the Joyful, Sorrowful and Glorious Mysteries and meditations for the Luminous Mysteries from the Book of Proverbs, the wise words of Solomon. The 20 Mysteries of the Most Holy Rosary open with a New Testament reflection. There is a short Scripture meditation from either Psalms or Proverbs for each Hail Mary. An Old and New Testament icon from Julius Schnorr von Carolsfeld's Treasury of Bible Illustrations accompany each mystery.

His Sorrowful Passion This prayer book integrates Sacred Scripture meditations with the prayers of the Chaplet of Divine Mercy. There are two Scriptural Chaplets: one chronicles Jesus' Passion and the other features the Seven Penitential Psalms. The woodcuts of the 15th century Catholic artist, Albrecht Durer, illustrate this book.

From Genesis to Revelation: Seven Scriptural Rosaries This prayer book is the most thorough and extensive collection of Scriptural Rosaries you will find anywhere. This prayer book goes well beyond the traditional Scriptural Rosary and penetrates the heart of the meditative spirit of the mysteries. It addresses many dimensions: time, from the Old to the New Testament; authors, from Moses, Isaiah, to the Evangelists; and perspectives, form the purely historical to deeper spiritual and prayerful insights. Those who pray the Rosary and those who read the Bible will equally find this prayer book inspirational.

RECORDED PRAYERS AVAILABLE ON CD

The Sanctity of Life Scriptural Rosary (2nd Ed. with Luminous Mysteries) Sacred Scripture selections prayed with the Most Holy Rosary uniquely brings you God's message of the dignity and sanctity of life. The prayers are accompanied by meditative piano music. Four different readers lead you in more than two hours of prayerful meditations. Includes four songs from the composer and soprano Nancy Scimone, winner of the UNITY Awards 2002 Best Sacramental Album of the Year for ORA PRO NOBIS. Includes 16-page book with the complete text of the Sacred Scripture selections. Double CD. CD 1 includes the Joyful and Luminous Mysteries and CD 2 includes the Sorrowful and Glorious Mysteries.

Time for Mercy Composer and singer Nancy Scimone offers you a new, spiritually uplifting Chaplet of Divine Mercy melody. This Scriptural Chaplet of Divine Mercy is based on the Penitential Psalm Scriptural Chaplet of Divine Mercy from the book, His Sorrowful Passion. Brother Leonard Konopka, MIC, prays selections from the Seven Penitential Psalms, while Nancy Scimone's crystal clear soprano voice brings us God's message of Divine Mercy.

Quantity orders of Suffering Servant Scriptorium books or CDs may be purchased for liturgical, educational, or sale promotional use. For discount schedule and further information, please call toll free 888-652-9494 or write to us at:

Suffering Servant Scriptorium
Special Market Department
PO Box 1126
Springfield, VA 22151